GIANT ANIMALS

CHINESE GIANT SALAMANDERS

Susan Schafer

Cavendish
Square
New York

Published in 2015 by Cavendish Square Publishing, LLC
243 5th Avenue, Suite 136, New York, NY 10016

Library of Congress Cataloging-in-Publication Data

Schafer, Susan, author.
Chinese giant salamanders / Susan Schafer.
pages cm. — (Giant animals)
Includes bibliographical references and index.
ISBN 978-1-62712-960-2 (hardcover) ISBN 978-1-62712-962-6 (ebook)
1. Chinese giant salamander—Juvenile literature. I. Title.

QL668.C24S33 2015
597.8'5—dc23

2013050646

Editorial Director: Dean Miller
Editor: Andrew Coddington
Copy Editor: Wendy A. Reynolds
Art Director: Jeffrey Talbot
Designer: Joseph Macri
Photo Researcher: J8 Media
Production Manager: Jennifer Ryder-Talbot
Production Editor: David McNamara

The photographs in this book are used by permission and through the courtesy of: Cover photo by Biosphoto/SuperStock; © Walter Myers, 4; © Walter Myers, 6; © Walter Myers, 7; Kelly Sweet/NATIONAL GEOGRAPHIC IMAGE COLLECTION/Getty Images, 8; Tim Zurowski/All Canada Photos/Getty Images, 9; Boston Globe/ Getty Images, 9; Tim Laman/National Geographic/Getty Images, 9; Geoff Brightling/Dorling Kindersley/Getty Images, 10; Ambre Haller/Flickr Open/ Getty Images, 12; Colin Keates/ Dorling Kindersley/Getty Images, 13; Wernher Krutein/www.Photovalet.com, 16; Best View Stock/Getty Images, 18; © NHPA/Photoshot, 18; Joe McDonald/Visuals Unlimited/Getty Images, 19; Wernher Krutein/www.Photovalet.com, 20; Courtesy of Egon Heiss and Royal Society, 21; Wernher Krutein/www.Photovalet.com, 23; Nature's Images/Photo Researchers/Getty Images, 24; © Juan Manuel Renjifo/Animals Animals—All rights reserved, 25; TOM MCHUGH/Photo Researchers/Getty Images, 26; Gary Meszaros/Visuals Unlimited/Getty Images, 29; V31S70/File:Andrias japonicus pair.jpg/ Wikimedia Commons, 30; Biosphoto/SuperStock, 31; © Ken Lucas/ardea.com, 32; Biosphoto/SuperStock, 33; © Natural Visions/Alamy, 34; Accurate Art Inc., 36; IMAGEMORE Co, Ltd./Getty Images, 39; ChinaFotoPress/Getty Images, 40; © Ringo Chiu/ZUMAPRESS.com, 41.

Printed in the United States of America

CONTENTS

CHAPTER ONE

GIANTS FROM THE PAST

Imagine all of the land around you void of life. Not a single tree. No birds, no bugs, no people. You are looking at prehistoric Earth more than 3.5 billion years ago. The oceans of the time were just springing to life with microscopic **organisms**, but it would be billions of years more before the first primitive plants, what we now call **algae**, would creep from the sea to form slimy mats along the oceans' edges. Not until around 400 million years or so ago would plants become fully **terrestrial**, leaving the sea behind.

A Prehistoric Giant

The ancestors of insects, centipedes, and spiders would follow the plants, feeding upon them and each other. The land was open and ready for more advanced animals to survive successfully. There was food to eat. There was shelter. There was fresh water. By then, the oceans were teeming with fishes, but how were they to get out of the water? How were they to breathe the air? How were they to keep their bodies from drying out in the air? Small changes and **mutations** in the **DNA**—the genetic instructions that give organisms their characteristics—of the ancient fishes would provide the answer.

Some fish developed stronger bones that would be able to support their bodies out of water. Their fins became more lobed. Lobed fins are fatter, more like pudgy clubs rather than thin, like swim fins. Lobed fins allowed the ancient fish to drag their bodies out of the water's edge to capture food along the shore. Because there were no other organisms competing for the same food source, these fish survived and passed on their new genetic traits for living on land to their young.

Eventually—around 390 to 360 million years ago—the **pectoral** and **pelvic** fins became the front and rear legs, and the so-called lobe-finned fishes became fully terrestrial **tetrapods**. Tetrapods are four-footed animals. One of the first tetrapods to "walk" on land about 375 million years ago was an amphibian called *Ichthyostega*. It had toes on the ends of its stubby legs. It did not have gills or scales. However, it still had a big head and body compared to its legs, so it wasn't the best walker, either. It would have been more like you lying on the ground and pulling your body along with your elbows.

Primitive plants colonized the land around 400 million years ago.

One of the earliest tetrapods and a descendent of the lobe-finned fishes, *Ichthyostega* feeds along an ancient shoreline.

Of course, many other genetic changes took place over the next few million years. Some primitive tetrapods moved into swamps and lakes, where the oxygen levels were much lower than in the oceans. Genetic changes in the DNA gave them lungs that allowed them to gulp air at first, and over time to breathe air when they were out of the water. Further changes took place in the skin. Fish-like scales were replaced by mucous-producing **glands**. Mucous glands helped the animals stay moist in the open air.

The early tetrapods did not, however, live far from water. They still laid their jelly-coated eggs in the water. Their eggs still hatched into little gilled "fish," or fishlike **larvae**, that would later change into the adult form. The ancestors of modern-day amphibians had arrived on Earth.

Now, imagine the land is covered with trees and many kinds of plants. Freshwater streams rush down the mountainsides. A huge, muddy brown tetrapod lumbers along at the water's edge. Its flat, heavy head moves from side to side with each slow step of its stubby legs. Its long tail drags along behind. Are you still envisioning prehistoric Earth? No way. You are in China today, watching the world's largest living amphibian, the Chinese giant salamander. Because it has changed little from its prehistoric ancestors, it is often called a living fossil.

Giant salamanders, such as this Japanese giant salamander, can grow to the size of some human adults.

Double Life

The word amphibian comes from the Greek words *amphi*, which means "of both kinds," and *bio*, which means "life." An amphibian leads a double life both in and out of the water. Early on, scientists used the word to include animals such as sea lions and otters, but now it is used only to refer to the class *Amphibia*: those animals between the fish and reptiles that are called salamanders, caecilians, and frogs.

Around 3,900 species of amphibians live on Earth today. However, scientists now know that the term amphibian doesn't really apply to many of them. The Chinese giant salamander is aquatic for its entire life, although it can move around out of water if it needs to. Some amphibians never leave the water at all. Others never enter the water, living only on land or in the trees. The Chinese giant salamander lays its eggs in water and has an aquatic larval stage, but not all salamanders do. Some lay their eggs on land, and these eggs hatch straight into tiny, land-dwelling amphibians.

A. A typical salamander has smooth skin, a long body, a tail, and when present, short legs.

B. A typical frog has smooth skin, a short body, and no tail.

C. A typical caecilian looks more like an earthworm than an amphibian.

The Chinese giant salamander, along with all other living salamanders and amphibians, belongs to the subclass *Lissamphibia*. *Lissamphibia* means "amphibians with smooth skin," from the Greek word *liss*, or smooth. The earliest ancestors of amphibians still had the scale-like skin of the fishes. Today, the Chinese giant salamander, other salamanders, and frogs have no scales. However, their modern cousins, the wormlike caecilians, have remnants of fishlike scales buried in their skin. Because the caecilians burrow underground, the scales help protect their skin from being scraped.

All salamanders, including the Chinese giant salamander, belong to the order *Caudata*. In Latin, *caudata* means "having a tail." Around 600 species of salamanders live around the world today, mostly on the northern continents. Their tail distinguishes them from the order *Anura*, which includes the tailless amphibians, the frogs.

The skeleton of a young giant salamander has a long body and many bones in its tail. Behind it, the skeletons of two different frogs show a short body without a tail.

Hidden Gills

The order *Caudata* contains nine families of salamanders. The Chinese giant salamander and its **extinct** relatives belong to the family *Cryptobranchidae*. The name *Cryptobranchidae* comes from the ancient Greek words *kryptos*, which means "hidden," and *branchion*, which means "gill." They are called hidden gills because the gills of the larvae are lost in the adults, leaving only gill slits behind. The gill slits look like slices cut through the skin at the back of the head.

The family includes three living species: the Chinese giant salamander, the Japanese giant salamander, and the North American hellbender. The hellbender's name comes from old stories about how these creatures bent the gates of hell to get through and live on Earth. A lot of people think the Chinese giant salamander is ugly enough to have gotten here the same way.

When the Chinese giant salamander was discovered, scientists assigned it a **binomial**, or two-part, scientific name. Every organism on Earth, living or extinct, has its own unique binomial name. Scientists use binomials based on Greek and Latin words so that any scientist around the world can understand what another scientist is talking about, even if they don't speak the same language. The first part of a binomial is the genus, which is more general. The second part of the binomial, the species, is more specific. The scientific name for the Chinese giant salamander is *Andrias davidianus*. The Japanese giant salamander is *Andrias japonicas*, and the hellbender is *Cryptobranchus alleganiensis*. Three additional members of the family are extinct. One of them was a species of Andrias that was a close relative of the Chinese giant salamander.

CLASSIFICATION SYSTEM

Scientists classify plants and animals in order to give each one a unique name and to group them according to their shared characteristics. The largest group is the kingdom. For example, all animals, including the Chinese giant salamander, belong to the animal kingdom. The smallest group is the species. A species is grouped by characteristics that are unique to one particular type of organism but are not found in any other species.

Classification of the Chinese giant salamander:
Kingdom *Animalia* (animals)
  Phylum *Chordata* (chordates)
   Class *Amphibia* (amphibians)
    Order *Caudata* (tailed amphibians)
     Family *Cryptobranchidae* (giant salamanders)
      Genus *Andrias* (manlike salamander)
       Species *davidianus* (pertaining to zoologist Armand David)

As the largest living amphibian, the Chinese giant salamander is also the largest living salamander. It has been known to reach lengths of nearly 6 feet (180 cm). That is within the range of height for most human adults. In fact, the Chinese giant salamander is so large that when the first fossil of its closest ancestor from eleven to five million years ago was discovered in 1726, it was believed to be a human that had drowned in the biblical flood. At the time, it was named *Homo diluvia*, from the Latin words *homo*, meaning "human," and *diluvia*, meaning "of the flood." The scientific name for living humans is *Homo sapiens*, meaning "wise human."

When the large, fossilized bones of a giant salamander were first discovered nearly three hundred years ago, scientists at the time believed they were the remains of a human.

It would be over a hundred years later before scientists finally figured out that *Homo diluvia* was actually an extinct species of giant salamander. It was renamed *Andrias scheuchzeri* in the early 1800s, from the Greek *andrias*, which means "image of man," and *scheuchzeri*, in honor of its discoverer, Johann Jakob Scheuchzeri. It grew to lengths of more than 7.5 feet (230 cm). That's longer than the tallest player ever inducted into the Basketball Hall of Fame.

This giant salamander fossil was found in what we now call Europe. It is the closest known relative of the ancestral line that gave rise to the Chinese giant salamander, which is now found only in small areas of China. Before the Earth went through a severe drought, or dry spell, about sixty million years ago, giant salamanders were found all over what are now the continents of Eurasia and North America.

It is not that surprising that an animal such as the Chinese giant salamander would be thought to be human because we are actually very much alike. We both belong to the phylum *Chordata*, which includes fish, amphibians, reptiles, birds, and mammals. The chordates, from a Latin word which means a cord or string, have a backbone containing a nerve cord. In humans, the nerve cord becomes the spinal column and forms our central nervous system.

Humans and the Chinese giant salamander are both vertebrates of the subphylum *Vertebrata*, which are chordates with backbones. We share most of the same bones and organs inside our bodies. We both even have gill pouches, but humans only have them for a short period when they are **embryos**. The gill pouches in the Chinese giant salamander become gill slits, while those of humans develop into the Eustachian tubes, middle ear, and tonsils.

And of course, humans and the Chinese giant salamanders are animals, belonging to the kingdom *Animalia*. Both our bodies are highly organized. They have eukaryotic cells, which are cells with DNA inside of a nucleus. These cells **differentiate** into many different kinds of tissues, organs, and organ systems, each with their own special functions. As organisms, both humans and Chinese giant salamanders are actually similar to all living plants and animals on Earth. All organisms take in food, which their bodies break down into the energy needed to run their bodies. They respond to stimuli in the environment, reproduce, grow, and develop. No wonder early scientists thought a giant salamander fossil was human.

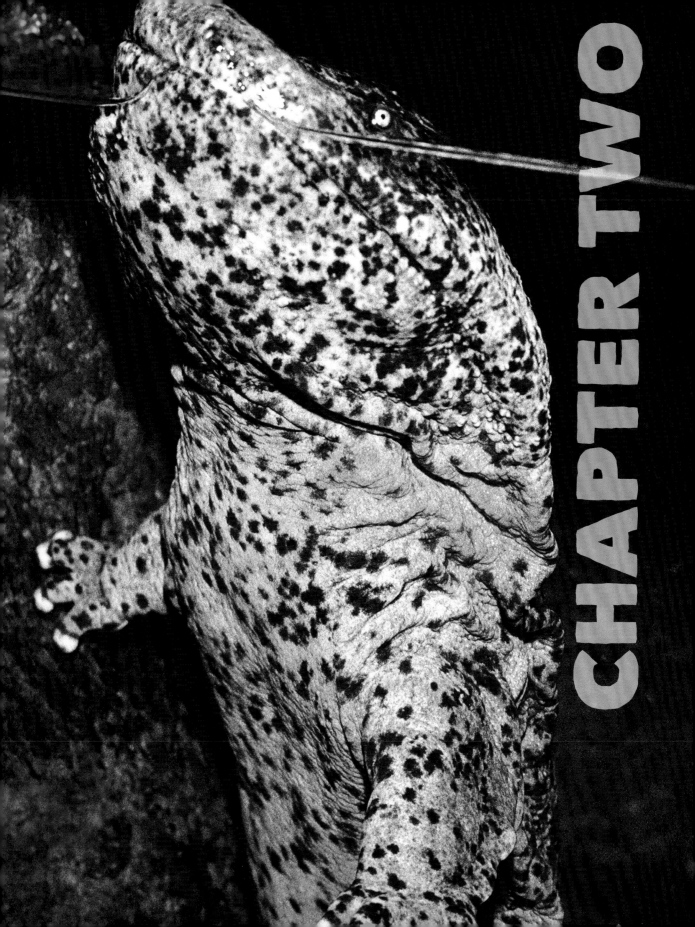

CHAPTER TWO

THE BODY OF A GIANT

All salamanders have the same basic shape, so it is easy to see that they are all related, however closely or distantly. They have sturdy bodies with four short legs. They have five toes on their back feet, and never have more than four toes on the front. They have a long rounded tail that makes up more than half of their total length.

The Basic Salamander, Modified

As with most animals, however, there are exceptions to the rule. The Chinese giant salamander looks more like its fishlike ancestors. Its tail is flattened from side to side and features a dorsal fin along the top. Its legs are very stubby, like its lobe-finned predecessors, and it is not a strong walker. While still husky, its body is flattened like a pillow, and it has a large, flattened head.

The Chinese giant salamander has small eyes positioned on top of its head so it can sense the movement of prey swimming above it. It has no eyelids, so it can't blink. Its eyes are kept moist by the water, so it doesn't need eyelids like the animals that live on land. Eyelids allow land animals to blink and moisten the surface of their eyes, like windshield wipers on a car window.

The Chinese giant salamander does not have sharp eyesight. Instead, it relies upon the senses of smell and touch to move around and find

The Chinese giant salamander has a flat head with tiny eyes and a tail that is flattened from side to side for swimming.

food in the dark, underwater areas where it lives. Its sense of smell also helps it pick up information about its environment, mates, and other competitive males.

Multipurpose Skin

The skin of the Chinese giant salamander is smooth and highly **glandular**, which means it contains many glands. A gland is a group of specialized cells that produce a specific substance, such as a **hormone**, mucous, or a poison. Mucous secreted by the skin helps keep this giant from drying out when it is not in the water. The mucous also makes the Chinese giant salamander slippery, so it is hard to grab and can more easily escape predators. Mucous also reduces friction and makes the salamander more streamlined when swimming.

Imagine yourself eating the food that you hate most. Are you making a face? Do you want to spit it out? Well, that's what Chinese giant salamanders' predators do. Poison glands in Chinese giant salamanders'

THE HELLBENDER

The Chinese giant salamander's smaller relative, the North American hellbender, is also called the snot otter because of its ability to secrete abundant amounts of mucous when grabbed. The slippery mucous helps ensure it won't be grabbed by a predator, and also protects its skin from scrapes, bacteria, and mold that might cause serious skin infections.

How would you like to have your own built-in bug repellent? Mucous also helps the hellbender repel parasites that might try to burrow into its skin. The snot-like mucous produced by the Chinese giant salamander also functions to protect it from predators, skin infections, and harmful parasites.

skin secrete a gooey substance that gives them a bad taste. The bad taste prompts predators to drop them if they are grabbed. Predators will also remember that bad taste the next time they see a giant salamander, so they won't try to take a bite.

Many salamanders are brightly colored as well, in hues of red, orange, yellow, or blue to remind predators that they are poisonous. It's like waving a warning flag. In some cases, the poison can make a predator sick or even kill it. Although Chinese giant salamanders are not brightly colored—they are in fact a muddy color—their skin secretions also give off a bad smell as an additional reminder to predators to stay away.

A Chinese giant salamander's skin is wrinkled and appears to be rough and bumpy around the head, neck, and sides. Long folds of skin run down the sides of the body. These bumps and folds increase the salamander's surface area. The larger the surface area of the skin, the more oxygen the salamander can absorb from the water. Essentially, the Chinese giant salamander breathes through its skin.

The Chinese giant salamander is able to breathe underwater through its wrinkled skin.

Terrestrial air-breathing animals also breathe through their skin—that is, the skin lining the inside of their lungs. Although the Chinese giant salamander primarily breathes through its outer skin, it also has lungs. Now and then, it will go to the surface of the water to gulp air like its prehistoric ancestors.

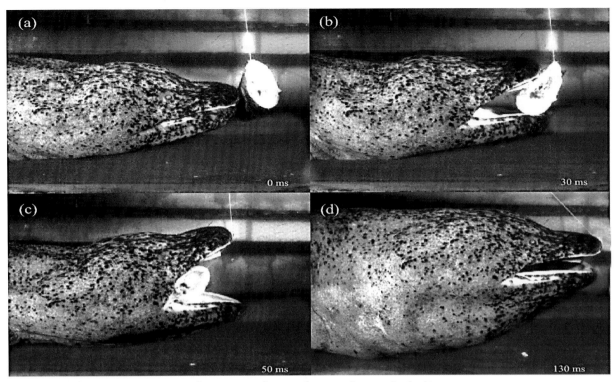

(a) 0 ms
(b) 30 ms
(c) 50 ms
(d) 130 ms

Like an underwater vacuum cleaner, a giant salamander sucks in its prey.

The bumps on the Chinese giant salamander's skin, called sensory nodes, are also able to pick up the slightest vibrations in the water. This trait was also inherited from its fishlike ancestors. Since it feeds mostly at night, the salamander uses these sensory nodes to sense the movement of its prey without having to see it. The Chinese giant salamander will eat just about anything that will fit inside of its gigantic mouth. This includes fish, insects, worms, snails, shrimp, crayfish, crabs, small reptiles and mammals, and even other giant salamanders!

When the Chinese giant salamander senses movement close to its mouth, it snaps open its jaws, causing water to rush into its cave-like throat. The suction that is created sucks in its prey with the rushing water, and its mouth snaps closed like a mousetrap. The Chinese giant salamander has a keen sense of smell, so it can also pick up the scent of its prey in the water.

In addition to providing an increased surface area, the Chinese giant salamander's skin is highly **vascular**. That means the skin contains small blood vessels, called capillaries, which come very close to the skin's surface. This allows the red blood cells inside of the capillaries to pick up oxygen more easily from the water. The oxygen is then moved through the bloodstream to all of the cells in the salamander's body. A steady supply of oxygen is needed by all living things so their cells can burn the sugar they get from their food. Burning sugar releases the energy needed to move, hunt, reproduce, and otherwise live.

The closer the red blood cells are to the source of oxygen, the more easily they can pick the oxygen up. It is a more efficient delivery system, just as it would be easier for people to hand a package to a mail carrier at their front door instead of having to chuck it onto the freeway and hope the driver gets it in all the traffic.

Lumps of Mud

The Chinese giant salamander is normally dark and muddy looking. Its skin is blotched and spotted with brown, green, and black. It looks more like a clump of mud or a slimy rock than a living thing. Its color gives it camouflage, helping it to blend into the river bottoms where it lives. A pink-skinned **variant** of the Chinese giant salamander has been bred by a farmer in China, although pink individuals would not normally live long in the wild. Pink skin would stand out like a neon sign, attracting the larger fish and other predators that might eat them.

Because its body blends in with the mud, plants, and rocks of its surroundings, the Chinese giant salamander doesn't have to hunt for its food. Instead, it just nestles down and waits for an unsuspecting meal to pass by. It saves a lot of energy by not having to go out and look for prey. In addition to saving energy by being a couch potato, it

The muddy brown, spotted skin of a Chinese giant salamander helps it blend into the bottoms of rivers and streams.

has a slow metabolism and is able to survive for weeks without eating. If nothing to eat swims by for a while, it is not a problem for the Chinese giant salamander.

From Giants to Pygmies

Today, salamanders come in all sizes. The largest Chinese giant salamander at 6 feet (180 cm) long could lie across the width of most driveways, or stretch all the way along a sofa. The Japanese giant salamander is only a little smaller, and can reach up to 5 feet (152 cm). Their smaller relative, the hellbender, grows to only about 2.5 feet (76 cm), which is still big for a salamander.

Weight-wise, the largest Chinese giant salamanders have been reported to weigh as much as 80 pounds (36 kg)—the weight of a large Labrador retriever—although most are not that heavy.

The eel-like, three-toed amphiuma has small, unusable legs. After the Chinese giant salamander, it is the next largest living salamander.

When it comes to salamanders, few come close in size to the Chinese giant salamander. The next largest salamander in the world is the three-toed amphiuma, which looks a bit like an eel. It lives in ponds, lakes, and streams in the southeastern United States, and grows to a maximum length of a little over 3 feet (91 cm). Think of the length of the standard ruler you might use in your math class at school, which typically measures 1 foot (30 cm). One amphiuma would be more than three school rulers long, but it would take two amphiuma, standing nose to tail, to be longer than a Chinese giant salamander.

The oldest giant salamander on record was a Japanese giant salamander that lived in a zoo for fifty-two years, so scientists believe that the Chinese giant salamander lives at least that long, if not longer.

Think about the size of the Chinese giant salamander, and then picture what it might look like next to the smallest salamander. *Thorius arboreus* is one of a number of Mexican pygmy salamanders. Most individuals of this tree-dwelling species are less than 0.8 inch (20 mm). If it weren't for its long tail, its body would be smaller than the power button on most TV remotes. Curled up, it would look just like another bump on the back of a Chinese giant salamander.

THOMPSON'S CAECILIAN

Only one other amphibian comes close to the length of the Chinese giant salamander. Thompson's caecilian from Columbia in South America reaches a length of around 5 feet (150 cm). Although that's as long as some Chinese giant salamanders, the caecilian looks much smaller because it resembles a long, skinny worm and only weighs a couple of pounds (less than a kilogram).

CHAPTER THREE

AT HOME IN THE RIVERS

While its ancestors lived in swamps or lakes, the Chinese giant salamander today lives in cold, rocky mountain streams and rivers where the water moves swiftly and is highly oxygenated. Moving about in waters ranging in temperature from a little above freezing to a little below room temperature, these salamanders seek out rock crevices, submerged logs, and other burrows to hide in during the day. At night, they come out to feed.

Den Masters

The Chinese giant salamander lives in the Zhu Jiang (Pearl River), Huang He (Yellow River), and Yangtze River of China, at elevations below 5,000 feet (1,500 meters). It is also found on the island of Taiwan, but scientists believe it was introduced there by people and does not occur naturally. Its cousins, the Japanese giant salamander and the North American hellbender, also live in larger, fast-moving rivers and streams.

Much information on the breeding of the Chinese giant salamander comes from what is known about the Japanese giant salamander and the hellbender, whose breeding habits in general are very similar. Courtship and breeding begins for the Chinese giant salamander in the late summer or early fall. This is unusual, because breeding for most salamanders is brought on by warm spring rains. Adult Chinese giant salamanders may take as long as fifteen years to become sexually mature, meaning they are ready to produce **sperm** or eggs.

The breeding season begins when the sexually mature adults migrate upstream to gather in nesting areas. In some cases, hundreds may gather in one area. Chinese giant salamanders, normally only active at night, are more likely to be seen during this time because they are moving around more during the day. They migrate upstream because the faster-moving water at higher sites better oxygenates the water, which in turn is better for the development of the eggs once they are laid.

A male clears out a large nesting chamber, called a den, under a rock or log and aggressively defends it against other males. Competing like gladiators, males are sometimes wounded during their battles. The winner becomes the "den master" of his chamber, keeping other males out while letting females in. Occasionally, a den master will allow another male in, but scientists aren't sure why.

A female is **gravid** when her body is enlarged with eggs that are ready to be deposited. One or more gravid females are attracted to a den by scent, or they may be driven inside by the den master. Chinese giant salamanders are one of the few salamanders that have a voice, but it is not reported whether they use their voice for breeding or to communicate with one another. Their vocalizations have been described as a whine, a croak, a hiss, and a baby's cry. In China, the giant salamander is called *wawa yu*, which means "crying baby fish."

Eggs Without Shells

Once inside the den, a female Chinese giant salamander will lay two long strings of eggs, like two pearl necklaces, side-by-side. She lays the strings of eggs in a clump the size of a grapefruit. Females may lay as many as 400–600 eggs in each clump. The eggs are soft and jellylike without a hard covering, like the egg white of a chicken egg without its hard shell. Each egg of the Chinese giant salamander is about 0.3 inches (7–8 mm) in diameter, about the size of a green pea. However, each egg is surrounded by several layers of jelly, which forms a protective capsule around it. With their jelly capsules, the eggs are more like 0.8 inches (20 mm) in diameter, or about the width of a nickel.

Looking like beads on a string, giant salamander eggs are protected by layers of jelly.

The eggs are fertilized externally by the male as the female is laying them. This means that he releases his sperm over the eggs, and **fertilization**—the joining of the egg and sperm—takes place outside of the female's body. **External fertilization** is considered to be a primitive trait because it is the same method used by the fishlike ancestors of amphibians. Most modern salamanders, having moved away from the aquatic environment and adapted to life on land, use a unique method of **internal fertilization** called sperm transfer.

In sperm transfer, the male deposits a spermatophore on the ground. A spermatophore is a cap of sperm on top of a little stalk, like a golf ball sitting on top of a tee. The female then walks over the spermatophore and picks it up with the opening through which she will lay her eggs. This opening for laying eggs happens to be the same opening through which the body wastes are excreted, which is also true for the Chinese giant salamander and for all other amphibians, reptiles, birds, and some

Unlike terrestrial salamanders, giant salamanders live and breed underwater.

primitive mammals.

In terrestrial salamanders that lay their eggs on land, the female usually watches over the eggs. However, in the case of the Chinese giant salamander, the male takes care of them. After fertilizing her eggs, the den master drives each female out of the den. In the end, he may have the egg masses of many different females.

Protective Parents

The male Chinese giant salamander will remain with the eggs for the next two or three months until they hatch, guarding them against any danger. If left unprotected, many predators, such as fish, insects, and even other giant salamanders, will eat the eggs. Movements of the male within the nest chamber increase water circulation and help to aerate the eggs. Scientists suspect that agitating the eggs also helps them to develop normally. Some salamander species will remove infected or dead eggs, but this behavior is not reported in the Chinese giant salamander.

Parental care takes place when any parent spends extra time and energy to take care of its young. This increases the chances that the young will survive. Parental care is not common in frogs and caecilians, but occurs in the majority of salamanders, usually in the form of tending the eggs. The Chinese giant salamander spends a few extra months caring for its eggs.

While still larvae, giant salamanders are already larger than most adult salamanders.

When the eggs of the Chinese giant salamander hatch in the early spring, the larvae look like miniature giants, except that they have gills. They are around an inch long (25 mm) or a little less. A bulging yolk sac below their bellies provides them with a rich source of food until they start feeding on their own about a month later. As a rule, salamanders tend to have larger hatchlings than other amphibians because of the larger yolk.

Once the larvae start hunting, they hunt as a group, like a little school of fish. Little is known about the larvae in the wild because they are rarely seen, but scientists assume that many are lost to predators. When the larvae reach around 8 or 9 inches (20 to 23 cm) in length, they begin to lose their gills.

A Big Baby

The larvae of the Chinese giant salamander have external gills. External gills grow from the outer surface of the gill slits and stick out on either side of the larvae's head. The gills are folded and feathery like little branching trees, which provide more surface area for picking up more oxygen out of the water. In fish, the gills are internal, inside the chambers under the gill slits. Water passes through the gill slits from outside of the body, bathes the gills in oxygen-rich water, and exits again.

Most salamander larvae will lose their gills and leave the water to become mature terrestrial salamanders, ready to reproduce. Chinese giant salamander larvae, however, lose their "outer" gills as their bodies grow and develop. They continue to grow until they are mature and able to reproduce, but they never lose all of their larval characteristics, and they don't leave the water. They still develop lungs and lose all of their external gills, but they also retain at least some of their gill slits. They never lose their larval teeth, or the fin on top of their tail. They never develop eyelids for living on land. Essentially, they become gigantic grownups in a baby's body.

Even though it has lungs for breathing air, the Chinese giant salamander remains aquatic throughout its life.

Scientists call this phenomenon **pedomorphism**, from the Greek *pedo* for child, and *morphe*, meaning "form." Complete **metamorphosis**, meaning "to change form," does not occur. Because the Chinese giant salamander shows pedomorphism, keeping some of its larval traits into adult life, it is considered to be a primitive species. It still has many of the same characteristics as the ancient pre-land-dwelling amphibians.

METAMORPHOSIS

The egg mass of a giant salamander.

Many different kinds of animals, such as insects and amphibians, like the Chinese giant salamander, go through metamorphosis. The process involves radical changes in body chemistry, body shape, and behavior as the animal moves from a larval stage to an adult form. During the early stages of metamorphosis in amphibians, the animal devours food like a living vacuum cleaner and grows significantly. Then the body begins to change, starting with the development of limbs and other adult structures, such as the lungs. The process ends with the reabsorption of the gills and, in frogs, the tail. During reabsorption, the body of the changing amphibian breaks down and reuses the components of the old parts.

CHAPTER FOUR

ON THE HEELS OF EXTINCTION

Because of human activities, the Chinese giant salamander, like so many plants and animals around the world, is in trouble. It is listed on the IUCN Red List as Critically Endangered, which means it is at extremely high risk of becoming extinct within the next twenty or thirty years. Its population size has already decreased by 80 percent in the last sixty years. Having survived on Earth for millions of years, it could disappear forever if steps are not quickly taken to protect it.

Giants in Trouble

The Red List is kept by the IUCN, which stands for the International Union for the Conservation of Nature. The IUCN is an environmental organization that works in cooperation with individuals, groups, scientific institutions, and countries around the world to determine the conservation status of the most threatened species found in nature. Based on the data, or information, that it gathers, it assigns those species a status on the Red List. The Chinese giant salamander is only one of more than 20,000 species that now appear on the IUCN Red List. The goal of the IUCN is to raise awareness about the plight of threatened species and to find solutions for saving them before it is too late.

Seven categories exist for the Red List: Least Concern, Near Threatened, Vulnerable Species, Endangered Species, Critically Endangered, Extinct in the Wild, and Extinct. At the lower end of the list, a species of least concern is facing problems but is still widespread and abundant enough that is does not yet qualify for a higher status. Each step up the list is a step closer to extinction. The Chinese giant salamander is only two steps away from becoming extinct. A species is extinct when there is no reasonable doubt that the very last individual on Earth has died.

Splitting a Population

To determine a species' status for the Red List, one of the things officials look at is how small an area the population is occupying, compared to what it used to be. For example, a species that once lived over thousands and thousands of square miles (or square kilometers) might be cut down to an area the size of a dozen football fields or less. Officials also consider how severely the habitat has been broken up into separate pieces. The Chinese giant salamander used to be found in eighteen different provinces over a large area of China. Now, its population has been broken up into a handful of smaller populations.

When populations such as the Chinese

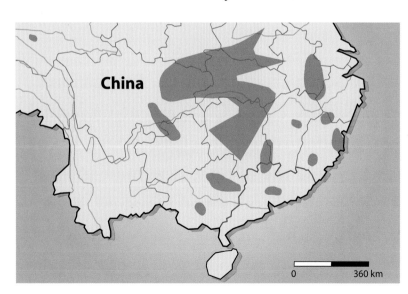

In this map, populations of Chinese giant salamanders are highlighted in orange. These huge creatures are now only found in a few pockets of habitat along China's rivers.

giant salamander become isolated, individuals can no longer reach each other for breeding. Mature animals have fewer choices in mates, so genetic diversity is lost. Genetic diversity is healthy for a population. It ensures that a large number of gene variations are being passed on to the next generation.

The characteristics that determine a species might be the same for all individuals, but individuals of the same species show many different types of a particular characteristic. For example, the human species has hair on top of the head, but individuals may have hair that is white, black, brown, blonde, or red. Even those colors have variations. Blonde might be platinum blonde, yellow blonde, honey blonde, dark golden blonde, or strawberry blonde. This is called genetic diversity.

The greater the genetic variation in Chinese giant salamanders, the more likely they will survive. For example, say a particular gene that protects the species against a disease has many variations in the population. If an outbreak of that disease hits, some individuals with "weaker" gene variations for fighting the disease may be lost. However, those with "stronger" gene variations for fighting the disease will survive. The species overall will not be lost.

On the other hand, now that the Chinese giant salamanders have become isolated, the smaller populations can no longer exchange genes with one another. If one of the isolated populations happens to have more of the weaker gene variation, it no longer has access to breeding with individuals with the stronger gene variation. The weak gene variation continues to be passed on, and over time, becomes more common. If that gene variation makes it harder to fight off a disease, and the disease hits, the entire population could be lost.

This is a very real concern for the Chinese giant salamander because a deadly virus has been spreading rapidly through captive populations that are being farmed for the Chinese meat market. Because some of the farmed animals have been released into the wild, scientists and many others fear that the virus could reach one or more of the isolated populations of Chinese giant salamanders with devastating results. At this point, it is unknown whether the virus has actually reached the wild.

Hunted to Near Extinction

The Chinese giant salamander is hunted for its meat and its body parts. The meat is considered to be a delicacy, and people will pay more than $300 a pound to eat it. Even though the salamander is protected in China, they are still heavily poached because they fetch such a high price. They are even poached in the nature reserves that have been set aside to protect them, and currently the Chinese government is not cracking down on hunters.

The body parts of the Chinese giant salamanders are also used in traditional Chinese medicine for treating illnesses, such as **anemia**. The challenge is trying to convince people to change their beliefs and see that there are other alternatives. Even when the salamanders are not being taken for food and medicine, fishermen who use crawfish and worms as bait to catch fish sometimes catch the giant salamander by mistake. They kill the salamanders for stealing their bait.

In fact, the Chinese giant salamander is disappearing so quickly that it has been ranked Number 2 on the Top 100 list of the world's amphibians that most need help. The Top 100 list is compiled by the Zoological Society of London. Only Archey's frog outranks it

Chinese giant salamanders are killed in order to use their parts for Chinese herbal medicine.

at Number 1. Like the Chinese giant salamander, Archey's frog is an ancient species, the most primitive of all of the frogs living today. Sadly, almost half of the entire world's amphibian species are declining.

For the Chinese giant salamander, not only is the population dwindling rapidly, the sizes of individuals within the population are getting smaller as well. Rarely do the giants reach the tremendous sizes that they once did in the wild. The majestic giants are shrinking by comparison.

Dirtying the Waters

As people take over more land to farm or build homes, more and more natural habitats are destroyed, not just for the Chinese giant salamander but for all of the plants and animals that live in the same area. When forests are cut down, rainwater runs off the cleared land and carries the soil with it. As the soil washes away, the water also picks up and carries harmful chemicals, such as pesticides, untreated sewage, fertilizers from fields and lawns, and rubber and oils from roadways.

BLOCKING THE RIVERS

Even without hunting and poaching, the Chinese giant salamander is threatened by habitat loss, or habitat destruction. It lives in areas of high rainfall, which often brings floods with it. Dams are built on rivers to control the flooding, as well as to collect water for towns and cities.

At the same time, the dams reduce the free flow of water in the rivers, which in turn decreases the amount of oxygen available for the salamanders to breathe. The dams also block the salamanders when they try to migrate upstream during the mating season, and destroy the places where they hide and breed.

Silt, which is the soil carried in the water runoff, and chemicals are then washed into streams and rivers, which pollutes the water. Silt causes water to become cloudy and lowers oxygen levels. Chemicals damage or kill the plants and animals that live in the water. Amphibians such as the Chinese giant salamander are particularly sensitive to pollutants because their skin is like a sponge, soaking up whatever is in the environment.

Saving the Giants

Many people are trying to save the Chinese giant salamander. Educational programs have been put in place at zoos, parks, and schools to teach people about the plight of the gentle giants. Zoos, parks, and universities are investing more money into research and conservation.

The Chinese giant salamander is now being farmed to meet the high demand for its meat. A number of large farms have been fairly successful at raising them up to their more normal historical size of 5 feet (152 cm) and 80 pounds (36 kg).

Zoo and aquarium exhibits of the Chinese giant salamander help people to learn about saving the endangered species.

Although the intention of farming was not to help the salamander, it has helped the wild populations by making it less profitable for poachers to hunt them. Farms are required to release a portion of their animals back into the wild to support conservation, but finding out what happens to them after they are released has been difficult.

Working with universities and zoos, scientists are studying the Chinese giant salamander both in captivity and in the wild. The more people know about the salamanders, the more likely they can be saved. New technologies are being used to locate wild populations and study their ecology and reproduction. Scientists take water samples in streams and rivers, and then analyze the samples for environmental DNA. Environmental DNA is the DNA in the mucous and body wastes that is shed by animals into the environment. Scientists then know where they are without even seeing them!

Land has been set aside as nature preserves to protect the rivers from poisons and silting by saving the trees and plants that grow in them. Special ramps and staircases have been built at dam sites so the Chinese giant salamander can continue to travel up and down streams and rivers during the breeding season.

Just as people have put the Chinese giant salamander in harm's way, it will be up to people to keep them from further harm and help in their recovery. One thing most people don't think about is that by protecting the giant salamander, as well as all other threatened plants, animals, and habitats on Earth, they are actually helping themselves. All people are part of the chain of life on Earth, and if the chain is broken, people will ultimately run out of space, food, and clean water. By saving the planet, people save themselves.

GLOSSARY

algae - a group of one-celled or many-celled plants, often growing in colonies, that have chlorophyll for photosynthesis, but no true leaves, stems, or roots; pond scum and seaweed are algae

anemia - a condition in which the body has too few red blood cells or the red blood cells do not work properly; anemia makes a person tired and weak

binomial - a two-word scientific name of a plant or animal that gives its genus and species

differentiate - to become different or distinct, especially by changing; stem cells differentiate into different kinds of cells, such as skin cells and blood cells

DNA - the genetic material found in all living cells that contains the information needed to function and reproduce; the abbreviation for deoxyribonucleic acid

embryo - an animal or plant that is just starting to develop; a salamander embryo grows inside of an egg

external fertilization - the fertilization of eggs outside of the female's body

extinct - having no living members of a species

fertilization - the joining of a sperm and egg to make a new cell that can develop into a new organism

gland - a group of specialized cells that produces a specific substance needed by the body

glandular - having glands

gravid - enlarged with or full of eggs or young

hormone - a chemical that is made by one organ in the body, travels through the blood, and affects certain target cells; insulin is a hormone produced in the pancreas

internal fertilization - the fertilization of eggs inside a female's body

larvae - the young of an animal that change their form during different stages of their lives; the larvae of frogs are called tadpoles or pollywogs

metamorphosis - change of form from embryo to adult

mutation - a change in the gene pattern on the DNA of an organism

organism - an individual living thing that is made of one or more cells

pectoral - of or relating to the chest

pedomorphism - retaining or keeping the characteristics of the young in the adult form

pelvic - of or relating to the pelvis or hip area

sperm - a male reproductive cell that carries a single copy of the genes of the parent

terrestrial - living on or in the ground

tetrapod - a vertebrate that has four legs or leg-like appendages

variant - different in some way from others of the same kind

vascular - consisting of vessels that carry blood

FIND OUT MORE

Books

Coborn, John. *Amphibians Today*. Neptune City, NJ: TFH Publications, 1997.

Cogger, H. *Reptiles and Amphibians*. London: Time Life UK, 1999.

Websites

ARKive

www.arkive.org/chinese-giant-salamander/andrias-davidianus

Discover facts, photos, and videos about the Chinese giant salamander and learn what makes it special.

BBC Wildlife Finder

www.bbc.co.uk/nature/life/Chinese_giant_salamander

Watch videos and learn the latest news about the Chinese giant salamander.

EDGE of Existence

www.edgeofexistence.org/amphibians

Learn about the life and habitat of the Chinese giant salamander.

Memphis Zoo

www.memphiszoo.org/chinesegiantsalamanderconservation

Read, look at photos, and watch videos about the Chinese giant salamander and learn what is being done to save it.

INDEX

Page numbers in **boldface** are illustrations.

ABOUT THE AUTHOR

Susan Schafer is an author, artist, and educator with a passion for animals. She has written numerous books about animals, including horses, turkey vultures, tigers, the Komodo dragon, and the Galapagos tortoise. The latter book was selected as an Outstanding Science Trade Book for Children by the National Science Teachers Association. Schafer has spent many years working in the field of zoology, including at the world-famous San Diego Zoo, where she acquired firsthand experience working with giant salamanders, caring for the Asian giant in captivity, and swimming the river bottom of the Current River in Missouri in search of the hellbender.